STEPHANIDES BROTHERS'
GREEK MYTHOLOGY
SERIES B: GODS AND MEN   **No. 10**

ORPHEUS AND EURYDICE

retold by MENELAOS STEPHANIDES
illustrated by YANNIS STEPHANIDES

translation BRUCE WALTER

DISTRIBUTORS FOR CANADA
ZIGRAS & ASSOCIATES INC.
131 HIGHGATE DRIVE
MARKHAM, ONT. L3R 3S6
TEL: (416) 609-1444 FAX: (416) 609-1445

SIGMA PUBLICATIONS
20, MAYROMIHALI ST., TEL. 3638941
GR-106 80 ATHENS, GREECE

ORPHEUS AND EURYDICE

Printed in Greece

1st edition 1980
2nd edition 1983
3rd edition 1987
4th edition 1989

Copyright © 1989: Menelaos Stephanides - Yannis Stephanides.
All rights reserved throughout the world.
ISSN 1105-249X
ISBN 960-425-024-8

THE MUSES AND THE GRACES

"In Athens, there was once a time when the statues outnumbered the inhabitants." With these words, a much-travelled author of ancient times tried to show how much fine arts like music, poetry, dancing, the theatre, painting and sculpture were loved in the Greece of long ago.

There was indeed such a time, a wonderful period when the people of that corner of the world called Greece believed themselves protected by the gods of Olympus — or, rather, a time when they believed themselves to be led by immortal artists.

For did not Athens itself choose as its protector the goddess Athena, she who is said to have first taught men the meaning of beauty and harmony? And was it mere chance that to Apollo, god of music, were dedicated the two most holy places in Greece, Delos and Delphi? What of Hephaestus, tireless master-craftsman; Dionysus, father of ancient drama and his followers, who were all musicians, singers and dancers? What of Pan, who made the hillsides and the forest glades echo to the sweet strains of his reed pipes? Take Hermes, even: as a new-born babe, his first thought was to fashion a lyre; and when he played it, he bewitched Apollo himself.

THERE WAS ONCE A TIME WHEN...

LOVE ONLY WHAT IS BEAUTIFUL

And to the ranks of these gods we must add the countless wood-nymphs and nereids whose dancing and song made every stream and sea shore of Greece re-echo with sweet melody.

And as if these divine beings were not enough to express the Greeks' love for the fine arts, there were also the Nine Muses and the Three Graces — all daughters of mighty Zeus.

The Muses were the goddesses who gave the world music, poetry, dance and drama, and with them they brought joy, laughter and tender feelings to the earth. In their hearts there was no place for sorrow, but only happiness and gaiety.

"Love only what is beautiful, scorn ugliness" was the nine sisters' advice, and thus they inspired men to create works of art.

The people of Mount Helicon said that Zeus' beloved daughters often came to the wooded slopes of their mountain, where shepherds heard their songs mingled with the chattering of the brooks and the chirping of the birds.

Even more often, the nine sisters were to be found at Delphi at the side of Apollo, or Master of the Muses, as the great god of music was also called.

When the golden-haired god lifted up his lyre and his fingers brushed its strings, the Muses would at once begin their song. Then, beneath the shady plane trees of the Castalian spring, the wood-nymphs and the Nereids would gather for the dance. And the Phaedrian rocks, which towered above the spring, would take up their lovely melodies and send them rebounding back and forth till all the slopes of Parnassus echoed the divine song.

But to please their father, Zeus, the Muses often stayed at his side and lulled him with their songs. At the symposia of the gods, on Olympus, their sweet and lovely voices sang of all that had passed, all that was passing and all that was yet to pass. They recalled the noble stock from which the gods had sprung — Mother Earth and Uranus, the boundless blue sky; they sang of the mighty deeds of the gods; then finally they joined their voices in a hymn of praise to their father, ruler of gods and men. And whenever they did this, a happy smile would spread across Zeus' face.

Yet they never forgot ordinary men, and their songs also praised those who, by their arts, their wisdom or their heroic deeds, had done honour to the human race.

With the coming of the Muses, the sufferings of mankind were greatly relieved. It is even said that when the Muses were born and music came into the world, some people were so bewitched that they sang day and night, and could not bring themselves to stop even to eat or sleep, but went on singing until they died. Yet death stole upon them without pain, and they did not descend into the dark kingdom of Hades. Instead they became crickets. And ever since, these tiny creatures have been troubled neither by hunger nor thirst, but live only for their song and go on singing until they die.

The crickets love the Muses dearly, and often, when we believe them to be singing, they are really deep in talk with the nine sisters. Among other things, they tell them about men — who loves poetry and who song, and who loves the Muses most of all.

Each of the nine sisters helped all artists according to the kind of art they loved. One inspired heroic songs, another hymns to the gods, and yet another dance and music.

THE NINE MUSES

Calliope was the first and most revered of the nine sisters. She was the Muse of epic and heroic poetry. It was Calliope whom Homer called upon in the first verse of the Iliad, with the words: "Sing, goddess, of the awful anger of Achilles." Artists adored her and drew her with a pen in her hand.

Erato was the next of the Muses. Her theme was love poetry and she played the lyre. Then came Polymnia, who was always shown with a

thoughtful look on her face. She was the Muse of sacred hymns. After her was Euterpe, with her twin pipes, the Muse of lyrical song.

Two other Muses were devoted to the theatre: Thaleia, who held a smiling mask in her hand, and was the Muse of comedy, and Melpomene, who carried a woe-begone mask and was the Muse of tragedy. Both of them were among the followers of Dionysus.

The Muse of dance was Terpsichore, and she, like Erato, carried a lyre.

The last two sisters concerned themselves chiefly with the sciences. They were Clio, Muse of history, whose song was the deeds of heroes and always carried a manuscript in her hand, and Urania, Muse of astronomy, who sang the glory of the stars and whose symbol was a globe.

These were the Muses: kind, hard-working and always ready to help man beautify his life.

But they were not alone in their efforts; for at their side stood three lovely goddesses who helped the Muses in their task, adding grace to beauty. And that is how they were named: the three Graces.

At the symposia of the gods they stood at Apollo's side, and when the divine notes of his lyre filled the palaces of Olympus, the three Graces and the nine Muses would spring to their feet to begin their dancing and songs.

But as soon as the revels on Olympus were ended, the Graces would hasten back to earth to be at man's side. Their task was a heavy but a noble one. They cast out cares, sweetened men's lives, and made happy events such as love, marriage and festivals even happier still. An ancient hymn says of them: "You make everything sweet and lovely. Thanks to you, poetry

THE THREE GRACES

moves the hearts of men. With your aid, men become beautiful, wise and brave."

Everyone spoke their names with love and respect. They were the charming Aglaia, Euphrosyne, who loved and protected poets, and Thaleia, who adored music. They were three sisters as simple and direct as children, as pure as the lilies of the dawn and as lovely as the blossoming spring. They were the darlings of the gods, beloved of poets and singers, a favourite subject of sculptors and painters.

ORPHEUS AND EURYDICE

In those distant days when the Muses and the Graces made men's lives lovelier, there lived a great singer, poet and player whose name was Orpheus.

If anyone had asked, then, who was the most famous man in the world, he would not have been given the name of some king, or some great general or mighty hero. "No," the answer would have been: "Orpheus is the best-known and best-loved man in the world today."

THE MOST FAMOUS MAN IN THE WORLD

The most incredible tales were told of Orpheus, and the magic powers of this singer and his songs.

One only had to say: "I have heard Orpheus" and a crowd would gather, envious and admiring, demanding to hear of the great singer and his entrancing voice, the like of which the world had never heard before.

"Is it true," people would ask, "that when Orpheus sings the birds fall silent and the wild beasts gather around him? Is it true that his voice can move stones and that even the trees tear themselves from the ground and walk on their roots to be near him?"

ORPHEUS AND HIS SONG

And the answer would always be the same, confident and convincing: "When you, too, hear the voice of Orpheus, you will believe all that and much more besides. If you go to the town of Zoni, in Thrace, ask them to show you the oaks of Orpheus, which is the name they give to a group of trees that really look as if they are dancing. The trees have remained in that position ever since they heard Orpheus singing and playing his lyre. Orpheus' song can even calm the raging sea, and his voice is so strong it can be heard over the roar of Zeus' thunderclaps."

Such tales and many more were told of the great singer and, indeed, whoever was lucky enough to hear him — even if it was only once — immediately believed all the stories he had previously been told.

Orpheus was born in Thrace. His mother was the Muse Calliope and his father Oeagrus, king of Thrace. It was from his mother he inherited his love of poetry and song. His lyre was a gift from the god Apollo, and he was taught the art of playing it by the Muses themselves.

Lyre in hand, Orpheus would wander from village to village and town to town, singing in palaces and hovels alike. He sang of love, the mother of life, recounted the mighty deeds of heroes and sang the praises of those who had given their lives in noble causes.

Though his music filled his hearers with feelings beyond the power of words to describe, none was as moved, and none took greater pleasure in them than Orpheus himself. When he played to a large audience, Orpheus literally battled to achieve perfection. He wore himself out, suffered untold agonies, but always attained the unattainable. And then he would feel the overwhelming pleasure which was the reward for his noble efforts.

But every delight Orpheus had ever known was transformed into a happiness more wonderful still from the day he married Eurydice and they became the best-matched and most loving couple the world has ever known.

Aphrodite's winged son, Eros, had succeeded in binding the young couple in that loveliest of bondage, the ties of great and pure love.

Orpheus' art now soared to new heights. "There is nothing more lovely than true and well-matched love," he sang; and thanks to Eurydice his tender feelings, rooted in the joy of their shared lives, blossomed and flowered in countless unforgettable melodies.

Like all lovers, Orpheus and Eurydice sometimes wanted to be alone, to wander far afield and enjoy each other's company without a care in the world. They would often sit on a lonely hillside, and as they gazed on the lovely scenery spread below them, Orpheus would take up his lyre while Eury-

ORPHEUS AND EURYDICE

dice sang softly of the great and endless love which had brought them such happiness.

One day the young couple were strolling in the Vale of Tempe. The beauty of their surroundings was breathtaking. On the one side loomed the towering peaks of Olympus and on the other Mount Ossa, while between the two flowed the peaceful waters of the River Peneios, its banks overhung by age-old sycamores. Sitting in the deep shade at the foot of one of these trees, Orpheus leaned against its trunk and strummed the strings of his lyre while Eurydice danced and sang without a care in the world, only breaking off to chase after butterflies or gather wild flowers. Above their heads, the birds chirruped gaily and little wild animals frolicked and gambolled around their feet as if they wanted to show their joy at being in the company of such a loving couple.

Orpheus and Eurydice felt as if they could stay in that spot for ever. Their hearts overflowed with joy at the loveliness around them. They wanted to reach out and embrace all nature. The gods, it seemed, had given the young lovers a more than generous share of happiness.

Alas! That happiness would soon be bitter ashes. For those three stern sisters, the Fates, had decided that here the lovers' idyll must end. The thread of life which Clotho had woven for Eurydice stretched only to this point, and the lot which her sister Lachesis had picked out warned of a poisonous bite in the hour of Eurydice's greatest happiness.

And stern Atropos, who never permits the slightest change in what her sisters have decreed, wrote down Eurydice's cruel fate unmoved, in letters that could never be unwritten.

Why such unfairness?

Do the gods not know that when the greatest happiness is shattered its place is taken by the most unbearable grief? Why should such harsh blows fall on those who deserve reward, not punishment?

But it seems that the gods have their own concerns, and cannot always watch over the petty affairs of mortals.

For while Eurydice skipped and danced happily around Orpheus as he played his lyre and sang, she stepped, without realizing it, on a snake's lair. And immediately a great snake darted out and sank its fangs into her foot.

Eurydice gave a heart-rending cry. Orpheus broke off his song in mid-note and ran to his beloved with cold fear striking at his heart.

THE GREAT INJUSTICE

THE DEATH OF EURYDICE

The sight that greeted him was worse than his eyes dared believe: the pallor of death was spreading rapidly over Eurydice's face. She stretched out her arms in a despairing attempt to cling to her lover, but the poison had already coursed through her veins, and before Orpheus could take her outstretched arms in his, his darling Eurydice fell dead upon the ground.

Thus, in a single moment, a dream was shattered. Eurydice went down to the underworld, to the terrible kingdom of Hades, and Orpheus was left alone, unable to bear the pangs of his intolerable suffering.

Nothing could console him for the cruel loss of his beloved. As for his lyre, while its notes were too weak to bring him consolation, they were more than powerful enough to make his grief overflow. Whenever he picked up the instrument, his fingers plucked savagely at its strings, producing wild chords like thunderclaps in a raging storm, the outpourings of all the great singer's desperate unhappiness.

Nine days passed and nine nights, and nothing could soften Orpheus' terrible misery. And on the tenth day a thought took root in his mind that no mortal upon earth had ever dared to think before: he would descend into the

dreadful kingdom of the shades to bring back his loved one.

A mere singer is no Heracles, perhaps, and hardly merits the name of hero. Yet the love of Orpheus for Eurydice and the cruel way he had lost her gave him the courage and the daring of a second Heracles — courage to attempt the impossible. He resolved to go down into Hades while still alive and beg Pluto, king of the underworld, for the return of the one who had been so unjustly taken from him: his Eurydice.

Armed only with his lyre, he set off on a journey too fearful for most men even to contemplate.

He searched far and wide. He asked wise men and seers — but they all shook their heads:

"No, Orpheus, do not go. Dark Hades is not for the living."

"Even the dead find it hard to bear, and they all long endlessly to see the light of day once more."

"Pluto is stern and unbending, and Cerberus, who keeps ceaseless watch over the gates of the underworld, will never let you bring your loved one back again."

"You are not the only man in the world to lose someone he loved, Orpheus. Many have wept before you; many have felt that the pain of their loss would tear them apart; but little by little time dried their tears and healed their wounds. Man's fate is a hard one, and there is no-one who can change it."

A BOLD DECISION

WHERE ARE YOU GOING, ORPHEUS?

But Orpheus paid no attention to any of this.

"That was not the answer I was seeking," he would reply. "Show me the road which leads to Hades."

And so, by repeated questioning, he learned that on the flanks of Mount Taygetus, in the Peloponnese, there is a gorge leading to a dark cave which Heracles had once descended into to bring up Cerberus, the unsleeping guardian of Hades, a hideous three-headed dog with a tail which ended in a dragon's mouth.

It was a fearsome path that led to the underworld. The closer Orpheus got to the gorge, the wilder and more deserted the countryside became.

The last man whom Orpheus saw on his way called out to him:

"Hey! Where are you going? Turn back! No mortal ever takes that road, and no man ever steps inside that gorge. We would rather not set eyes on it, or even think about it."

But Orpheus entered the gorge and pressed on between the towering crags as if he had not heard a word. It was a landscape in which nothing grew but thorns and no creatures lived but snakes, but the strength of his love for Eurydice gave Orpheus the boldness and determination he needed to step over the threshold of Hades.

The further Orpheus went, the bleaker and more unwelcoming the scenery became, but he continued on his way until he reached the end of the terrible gorge and found himself facing a yawning black hole.

Any other man would have recoiled on seeing the fearsome gate of Hades, but Orpheus pressed on resolutely, and passed from the brightest daylight into the deepest darkness.

He had not gone forward many steps before he felt his hand caught in a firm grasp, and at the same moment an unearthly light sprang up around him. Turning his head, he saw a handsome man who held a rod round which were twined two snakes. On his head he wore a winged cap, and there were wings on his heels, too. Orpheus realized that the figure at his side was Hermes, the god who often came at Zeus' orders to lead the dead down to the underworld.

"I admire your courage, Orpheus," said Hermes, "but you have set out to achieve the impossible. The king of the dead is hard and unyielding and does not know the meaning of human pain. True, he lets Adonis return to earth every spring, but only because he is loved by Aphrodite, and even so he takes him back again each autumn. He makes no other exceptions, unless you include Persephone, his wife — and anyway, she is not dead, but an immortal goddess who returns to her mother each year by order of Zeus himself. So do not hope for that which can never be. Let me lead you back to the world of men."

"Lead me to Pluto, the king of Hades," was Orpheus' reply. And in his voice there was such determination that Hermes stood in silence for a moment, and then led Orpheus onward again, still holding his hand.

Their path led through a long cave which went down and down. They went on for hours, winding ever deeper into the bowels of the earth.

ORPHEUS
DESCENDS
INTO
THE UNDERWORLD

CHARON FERRIES A LIVING MAN

At last, through the utter silence that reigned around them, came the faint, rhythmic sound of water lapping against rocks. Orpheus peered ahead and saw that they were approaching the banks of an underground river. It was the Styx, the sacred river of Hades.

A ferryman was rowing his boat across the water towards them. This was Charon, come to pick up the shade of Orpheus (or so he thought) and ferry him over to the kingdom of Pluto on the other side. But when he saw a living man, he was so taken aback that he cried out angrily to Hermes:

"Don't you know that I take no living passengers aboard my boat! What have you brought him here for?"

"It was my own decision to come here," replied Orpheus boldly. "Now, will you be kind enough to let me over? I wish to appear before the king of the underworld."

"And I know why," retorted Charon. "So you can plead with him and beg favours. I wonder why you went to the trouble of such a journey, when you know you're no more likely to persuade me than you are my master, Pluto. Now, get out of my sight before I give you one with my oar and make you wish you'd never been so insolent. Go back to the world above and wait your turn to die, if you want me to carry you over."

While Charon was addressing these angry words to him, Orpheus unslung the lyre from his shoulder as if he had not heard, and brushed his fingers across its strings. Never before had the dark halls of Hades echoed to such bewitching notes.

"What sounds are these?" cried Charon in wonder, secretly hoping that Orpheus would go on playing.

And indeed, the hard-hearted ferryman had scarcely time to complete his thought before the notes of the lyre flooded the air once more, and Charon stood leaning on his oar as if a spell had bound him.

Then, never lifting his fingers from the strings, Orpheus moved slowly forward and stepped into the boat, followed by the wondering Hermes. Charon stood listening, motionless, for a few moments longer, then, raising the oar in both hands, he pushed off from the rocky shore and sent the boat gliding smoothly and silently across the sacred waters.

Entranced by the beguiling notes of Orpheus' lyre, Charon steered his boat over to the great gate of Hades, which loomed ahead. This gate always stood wide open, but it was guarded eternally by Cerberus. Hermes and Orpheus walked through. When Cerberus saw the god coming in with a living man, he could hardly believe his eyes. A deep growl welled from his three throats, and the dragon's head on the tip of his tail shrieked hideously. But

CERBERUS, GUARDIAN OF HADES

IN THE PRESENCE OF PLUTO

that was all; for the task of Cerberus was to prevent the dead from leaving, and not to close the gate on those who wished to enter.

Before long, Hermes and Orpheus were standing in the presence of Pluto, the god who ruled the underworld. He was seated on a tall, imposing throne. At his side sat his wife, the lovely Persephone, while on his left, on other raised thrones, sat the three wise judges of Hades: Minos, Rhadamanthys and Aeacus, whose task was to pass sentence on the dead for the crimes they had committed during their lives.

They all rose in surprise when they saw Hermes leading a living man into the underworld. Pluto's face darkened with rage, and he was about to hurl a furious question at Hermes when the superb strains of Orpheus' lyre filled the air, and the great singer's voice broke into a song of compelling beauty.

Pluto stood silent and ecstatic. The god whose ears heard nothing but the groans of the dead was now held spellbound by the voice of Orpheus himself, the greatest singer the world had ever known.

But if the sounds moved Pluto, they plucked an even deeper chord in Persephone's heart, bringing back memories of the lovely, flower-decked earth above, its bird-song and the babble of its crystal brooks, and of its singers who, with lyre and flute, made melodies to praise life's joys and give thanks to the gods.

The judges of the dead listened with the same hushed reverence, recalling the beauty of life in the world above. Stern Minos, the mighty king of Crete, was moved almost to tears. Just Aeacus, king of Aegina, choked back a sob; while Rhadamanthys, the great lawmaker and king of Boeotia, listened in ecstasy. Mighty lords though they might be in Hades, they knew how much happier was a slave's lot in the world above.

And so Orpheus sang on, his voice stirring waves of longing in his listeners' hearts. His verses told of the joys of life on earth, of love, the great gift of the gods, then they recounted his passion for Eurydice, and finally they poured out all his pain at the unjust loss of his beloved. And as his voice grew stronger, so did the emotions it aroused, spreading like ripples to the furthest reaches of dark Hades.

The shades of the dead heard Orpheus' heart-rending song and ceased their groaning. Tantalus, punished for his insolence to the gods by the pangs of hunger and thirst, forgot for a while his dreadful sufferings and listened spellbound. Sisyphus, who was paying the penalty of his evil deeds on earth by forever heaving a huge boulder up a mountainside, paused from his back-breaking labours to listen to Orpheus' song; and the Danaids, whose crimes in the world above now condemned them to pour water endlessly into a huge, bottomless urn, halted their futile task for a space and listened with bursting hearts.

THE LOVERS ARE REUNITED

But suddenly, from among the ranks of the dead, the shade of a young woman ran forward. It was Eurydice, who hearing Orpheus' song now flew to meet her loved one. And a moment later the law of untold ages was shattered: the shade of Eurydice threw itself into the arms of the living Orpheus.

Pluto looked on thunderstruck; for the act he now beheld was an open challenge to the sacred and eternal laws which separate the living from the dead.

And all who saw it feared that in an outburst of terrible rage Pluto would put a violent and horrible end to this scene of unheard of courage and beauty which they now witnessed.

Deeply moved, but fearing that Pluto's wrath would break upon him, too, Hermes begged the lovers to release each other from their passionate embrace. And the young couple at once did as he bid.

Now all eyes were on Pluto, waiting to see how the stern god's rage would vent itself.

Yet Pluto only hung his head and remained silent. After a long pause, he lifted it again and gazed at Persephone, whose lovely eyes were brimming with tears.

And then he turned to Orpheus and spoke:

"Tell me what favour you desire, and I shall grant it to you. I swear this by the holy waters of the Styx!"

"Mighty lord of the underworld," replied Orpheus, "I want you to give me back my beloved Eurydice. Her days in the fair world above were all too few, and when love came to her, she had no time to taste its joys. I cannot

bear to think of her suffering in the dark depths of Hades. I cannot live without Eurydice, nor she without me."

"It shall be as you desire, Orpheus, just as I promised. But you, too, must give me a promise in return."

"Whatever you wish, mighty lord", replied Orpheus.

"Eurydice may leave with you now. You will go ahead, and she will follow. But you will not turn your head to look at her before you reach the light of day. If you do so before then, Eurydice will return to my kingdom at that very instant."

Pluto's terms were hard, but Orpheus accepted them willingly, overjoyed to think that once they had climbed up into the sunlight again he would have won his loved one back for ever.

They set off. Hermes led the way, followed by Orpheus, while a little behind them came Eurydice. When they reached the gates, Cerberus reared his three heads threateningly, but as soon as Orpheus brushed his fingers against the strings of his lyre and its lovely melodies filled the air with their glorious notes, the fearsome guardian of Hades lowered his heads and stood silent and unmoving, bewitched by the sounds he heard.

Thus they passed through the gates of Hades, crossed over the Styx once more on Charon's ferry and started back up the long and rising path that led through the cavern. The way was hard and tiring, but none of them gave it a thought. Orpheus' thoughts were fastened upon Eurydice, who was following somewhere behind him. But was she following? This was the terrible doubt which slowly took root in Orpheus' mind. For in the silence of

AN ANXIOUS RETURN

21

death which reigned about them he could hear his own steps, he could hear the steps of Hermes going on ahead, but from behind he could hear nothing. Why?

"What if Eurydice is not coming? What if Cerberus would not let her pass through the gates of Hades? What if Charon refused to let her on board his ferry?"

"Ah, if only I knew that Eurydice were following me! If only I could see her or hear something!" The thought tortured him constantly all along the way. And the way was endless.

They were in thick darkness, but Orpheus could still make out the form of Hermes in front of him. If that were so, he only had to turn his head and he would be able to see if Eurydice were there behind.

"But what am I thinking?" cried Orpheus, as he realized where such thoughts were leading him. "Oh, Gods, if only I knew whether Eurydice is coming, and whether I shall see her when we reach the light! But I do not know. Why do I hear nothing? Nothing! Why?"

A prey to his fears, Orpheus followed in the footsteps of the god, his heart close to bursting with his terrible anxiety.

At last, a faint glimmer of reflected daylight appeared in the distance. Orpheus' anguish rose to breaking point. With each step, the light grew stronger, but as it did, so Orpheus' doubts grew more unbearable.

ORPHEUS LOOKS ON EURYDICE
Bright light now flooded the cave. Their journey was within moments of its end. Before them shone the light of day. Only seconds now, and Orpheus would have won his loved one back for ever. If she was behind him!

"And if she isn't?" thought Orpheus bleakly — and turned his head.

And saw Eurydice.

Ah, why are the gods so hard on man?
In an agony of despair, Orpheus stretched out his arms to embrace his loved one. But too late. Before he could touch her, she slipped from his grasp like a withered leaf caught by the autumn wind, and was whirled back to the dark kingdom of the shades.

This second loss was still more shattering than the first. Orpheus ran headlong after Eurydice in his desperation, but she had already vanished from his sight. Soon he found himself on the banks of the Styx once more and begged Charon on bended knees to carry him across. But he might as well have saved his breath, for the ferryman turned a deaf ear to his pleas. Seven days and seven nights he paced the banks of the Styx, pleading with Charon to row him to the other side, and on the eighth, vain, day he took the dark path once again and climbed the hard, steep way until he found himself once more in the light above, and in despair.

There, at the mouth of the cave, he found the lyre which had slipped from his nerveless grasp in that moment of horror when he had stretched out his hands to clutch at Eurydice. It was cruel beyond belief! The fallen lyre lay just two steps from the light of the sun!

**EURYDICE
IS LOST FOR EVER**

Orpheus bent down and took it up. Torn by grief, he crashed his hand across its chords, and the pain of his misery echoed and re-echoed through the savage mountains like a raging storm. Now, nothing could bring him consolation. Orpheus had lost his loved one for a second time because he could not accept the harsh terms imposed upon him by stern Pluto.

The unhappy singer returned to his homeland. Months went by, and then years, but Eurydice still haunted his waking dreams. Many people advised him to marry again, but in reply he would only pick up his lyre and play melodies so mournful that they broke the hearts of the very stones that echoed them.

At last, when the great feasts in honour of Dionysus were being held in Thrace, the time came for this great and tragic singer to meet his end.

THE GREAT SINGER DIES

The Dionysiac festivals were attended mainly by women, who drank till the wine spilled from their lips, and danced and sang in imitation of the Maenads, the wild nymphs of Dionysus' train. These women invited Orpheus to play and sing for them, but he was too miserable and sick at heart for dancing and such revels.

The women were offended by his refusal and left in anger, but when they returned from the festival, drunken and riotous, they met Orpheus on the road once more.

"Here's the fellow who insulted us!" they shrieked, "the one who hates us! the one who refused to honour Dionysus!" and with these words they began to attack him with rocks, with wooden staves, and even with sickles.

And so, their heads reeling from the fumes of the wine, hardly knowing what it was they did, they fell on the unhappy singer like savage beasts and tore him limb from limb.

When the women came to their senses and realized what a hideous crime they had committed, they went to the nearest river to wash the blood from their hands, and with it the shame of their deed. But the river suddenly dried up. The river god had led its waters away underground so he would not have to share in their guilt.

Orpheus died, but his soul sped gladly to Hades, where it was reunited with Eurydice.

Now Orpheus could at last gaze on his beloved with no fear that he might lose her once again. The joys of life were unknown in the dark kingdom of the shades; there was neither laughter nor joy in Hades, and no sound of lyre or melodious voice broke the silence of the underworld; yet Orpheus and Eurydice were happy there, if no one else was. For their love had defeated death itself.

And Orpheus' art, too, had won a similar victory.

On a wooded slope of Olympus, there is a spot where the birds sing more sweetly than anywhere else in the world. For it was here that the Muses buried Orpheus' body. But his lyre was borne by the waves to the island of Lesbos where it was washed up upon the shore, and, as the waves beat rhythmically against its chords, the lyre played sweet melodies. Its song was heard by Apollo, who came and took it up from the sea's margin and placed it high in the heavens; and ever since, it has shone as the bright constellation called The Lyre.

THE LYRE OF ORPHEUS SHINES IN THE HEAVENS

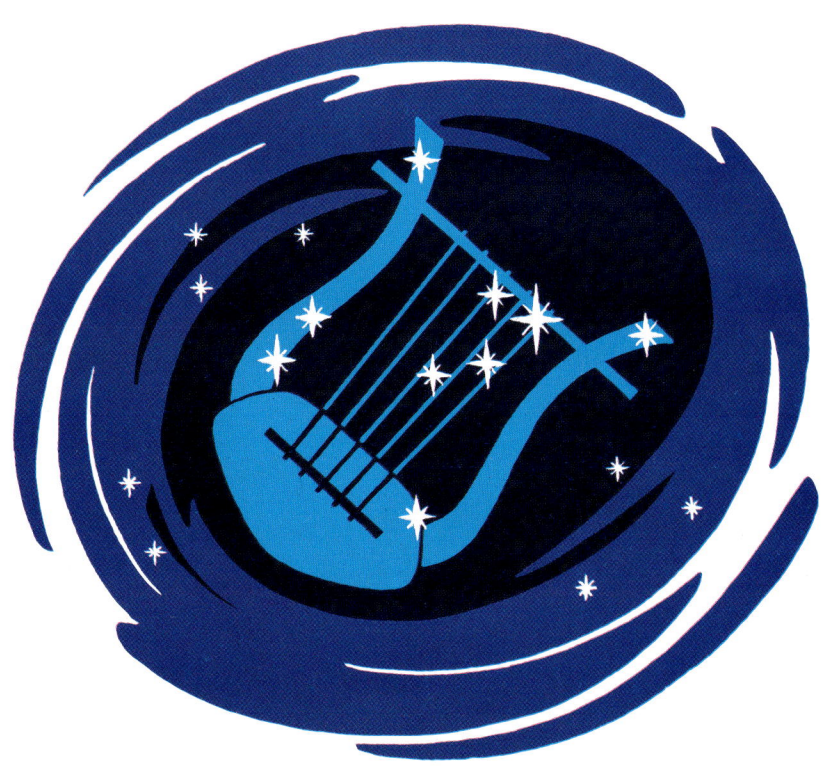

Years went by, yet still the waves kept up their sweet, rhythmic song as they beat upon the rocky headlands and the sandy coves of that lovely island. And this is why its people have kept their love of music and poetry, and have produced such great poets and singers as Sappho, Alcaeus and Arion.

ARION There is a delightful and unusual story about Arion which is well worth telling. According to this myth, Arion was the son of the god of the sea, the earth-shaker Poseidon. From his earliest youth he distinguished himself as a poet and musician, and one day he happened to catch the attention of Periander, ruler of Corinth and one of the seven sages of antiquity. Now Periander was a great patron of the arts, and when he heard Arion he was as entranced by his voice as by the verses of his song and his melodious playing. Deeply moved, he invited this marvellous singer to come to Corinth, which was then a rich and powerful city where artists of all kinds enjoyed Periander's generous support.

Arion accepted, and thanks to his move to Corinth he won such fame that soon his name was known in every corner of the earth.

One year, a great festival of the arts was held in Sicily. All the cities of the ancient world sent their brightest talent to compete, and Corinth chose Arion.

In Sicily, Arion's performances were a triumphal progress. Wherever he appeared he was wildly applauded. The judges never had any difficulty in deciding whom the victor's prize should go to. As composer, poet and player he won the first award in every town and festival he appeared at. And when the day came for him to return to Greece he had with him a whole treasury of gold cups and other gifts of priceless value.

But Arion was destined to fall among thieves. For the ship which was to carry him back to Corinth had hardly set sail when the captain, flanked by two burly sailors, marched up to the young singer and told him with a cruel laugh that they were going to throw him overboard.

"But what crime am I guilty of?" asked Arion in amazement. "What have I done to deserve such a fate?"

"If you really want to know, I'll tell you: you're carrying more gold than is good for you."

"As for the gold, you're welcome to it," replied Arion. "But at least spare my life, so that I can go on singing."

"We're not stupid enough to do you that favour," returned the captain. "For as soon as we reach Corinth you will tell Periander we have robbed you, and then it will be all up with us. Between you and me, I'd do the same thing myself if anybody were fool enough to strip me of my wealth but spare my life."

Yet even these harsh words did not make Arion lose hope.

"I see I cannot persuade you to grant me my life," he replied, "but you

ARION CARRIES OFF ALL THE PRIZES

ARION AND THE ROBBERS

must at least do me this personal favour: before I die, let me play my lyre one last time."

"Play, sing — dance if you like!" was the captain's callous answer.

And so Arion sat in the stern of the boat and began to play his lyre and sing, calling on his father, the great god of the sea, to come and help him.

The melody that wafted over the waves was lovely beyond belief, and soon a whole school of listening dolphins was following the ship. But the captain was quite unmoved by the song and suddenly gave the great singer a savage kick which sent him tumbling into the sea below. Then, without sparing a glance behind him, he made a beeline for Arion's sea-chest, anxious to set eyes on the treasure which had fallen into his hands — or which he thought had fallen.

For Arion had not drowned, after all. Seeing him sinking, one of the dolphins had immediately dived beneath him and borne his body up upon the waves. And soon the sweet airs of Arion's lyre rang out over the waters once more as the singer continued his voyage back to Greece seated upon the back of a dolphin.

The friendly creatures put Arion ashore at Tainaron in the Peloponnese and from there he managed to reach Corinth ahead of the robbers. As soon as he reached the city, he went straight to Periander and told him of his grim experience and how he had been saved.

The next day, the robbers' ship put into harbour and Periander summoned the captain to his palace to hear what had become of Arion.

The captain, of course, had rehearsed his answer:

"He wished to stay on in Sicily for a while, your majesty, and so we sailed without him."

"Do you swear to this?" asked the king. And what could the robber captain do but give his oath?

But at that very moment, a door opened and Arion appeared! The captain reeled in amazement. He could not believe his eyes!

"But this is not possible!" he gasped.

"And yet it is!" roared Periander. And he immediately ordered his soldiers to seize the man and bind him.

Bound hand and foot, the captain was thrown on board a ship which immediately put out to sea; and there, on Periander's orders, he was thrown over the side.

In his case, there was no miracle to save him.

ATHENA, THE FLUTE AND MARSYAS

While we are on the subject of music and musicians, here is one last myth — that of Marsyas the satyr, who lost his life because he dared to pit his skill in music against Apollo by challenging him with his flute.

But that flute had a story behind it, and if Marsyas had known the story, he would surely never have put the instrument to his lips. This is how the tale goes:

One day, the goddess Athena found the beautiful, long, thigh bone of a deer. It was a pleasing object, and she wanted to make something both attractive and useful from it. She soon decided what she would make, and began to work on the bone with great care and art. She cut off both ends, cleaned it out well inside and then drilled holes down its length. Finally, she fashioned a handsome mouthpiece at the top. When she had finished, she placed the mouthpiece between her lips and began to blow, placing her fingers on the holes and lifting them. Lovely sounds came from the instrument she had created. It was the world's first flute.

The goddess was enchanted with her new creation and never tired of playing it. On one occasion, however, when she was playing for the other gods of Olympus, she noticed that Hera and Aphrodite were staring at her and exchanging secret giggles.

Athena put down her flute and shouted angrily:

"Why make fun of me? Everyone else is enjoying my music, and you sit there laughing!"

"If only you could see your face when you blow into that thing, you'd understand why we're laughing," replied the two goddesses.

"They must be jealous of me," muttered Athena, and went off to play her flute by the banks of a river, where she could see her own reflection as she blew. But when she saw how her cheeks puffed out and her lovely face became distorted by the effort of blowing, she realized that Hera and Aphrodite could not be blamed for laughing behind their hands, and in a sudden burst of anger she hurled the flute away, shouting:

"Miserable toy! Because of you I am insulted. A curse on anyone who

picks you up and puts you to his lips."

The flute which Athena had thrown away was found by Marsyas, and, suspecting nothing of the curse, he picked it up, liked the look of it and decided to keep it. In time, he grew fond of the flute and learned to play it so well that whoever heard him said that not even Apollo could play as well.

How was unlucky Marsyas to know that the curse of Athena hung over him? He had never been one to boast, but now he began to tell everyone that he could make even better music than golden-haired Apollo.

It was not long before the great god of music appeared before the unlucky satyr. He was magnificently attired, and under his arm he carried his golden lyre. The nine Muses accompanied the shining god.

"How dare you call yourself a better player than me?" Apollo demanded. " Can there be anyone in the world, god or mortal, whose skill in music is a match for mine?"

"All we need do is put it to the test," replied Marsyas coolly. "Let your nine sisters judge which of us plays better. But whoever wins may impose any punishment he wishes upon the loser."

Foolish Marsyas, what rash words were these? Did you imagine that a mere satyr could pit his poor skills against a mighty god? And did you not know that the immortals are not to be insulted, and are cruel beyond belief when they wish to exact punishment? For Apollo's answer was swift and terrible:

"I shall defeat you and skin you alive for your insolence!" he screamed, his face flushed with rage.

But Marsyas seemed quite unconcerned, and putting the flute to his lips, began to play. The Muses stood listening in awe. Even Apollo thought his

MARSYAS CHALLENGES APOLLO

ears were deceiving him. For the music which flowed from Marsyas' flute was so perfect that neither god nor man could better it. Next, it was Apollo's turn, but though his music was as good as Marsyas' in every way, it was not better.

And so the Muses were unable to declare either of them the winner.

By now, Apollo was boiling with rage. He was determined to be revenged upon the satyr who had belittled him — by fair means or foul.

"Very well," he snarled, "now we shall play with our instruments upside-down!"

And holding his lyre the other way up, he played it as superbly as before. But a flute, alas, cannot be played with its mouthpiece pointing downwards, and poor Marsyas could not coax a single note from his instrument.

And so the Muses declared Apollo the winner.

The god's revenge came down on Marsyas like a thunderbolt, and the poor satyr died in hideous agony because he had dared to challenge an immortal.

The wood-nymphs wept for Marsyas and buried him by a river. The Muses felt sorry for the unlucky satyr and begged their father Zeus to take pity on him. The ruler of gods and men listened to their pleas, so Marsyas did not descend to the dark depths of Hades. Instead, his spirit was released into the waters of the river which flowed by his grave. Ever since, the waters of the river Marsyas have flowed as musically as if they were indeed playing a flute, and men have listened to its song with pleasure. But when the river remembers Apollo's cruel revenge, its waters swell with wrath and roar wild threats, spreading fear and sorrow in their path.

SOME ANSWERS TO POSSIBLE QUERIES

To those of our readers, young or old, whose reading of this mythology series may have prompted certain questions, we would like to say the following:

It is possible that you may have read the same myth elsewhere and noticed significant differences. This does not necessarily mean that one version is right and the other wrong. In their retelling, myths came to differ widely from place to place and from age to age and as a result several versions are now extant. In this work, we decided to give one version only, choosing either that most widely accepted, or the one we felt to have the most value. Working by the same criteria we have often added materials taken from other sources to round out a myth.

Another frequent cause of bewilderment are the contradictions generally encountered in mythology. For example, in one myth Zeus may be depicted as kind and fair, and in another tyrannical and unjust. Even Homer does much the same thing in the Iliad. At one point he has Thersites, a common soldier, lashing Agamemnon himself with the tongue of truth, while at another we see him crying like a child beneath the blows of Odysseus' gilded sceptre. These apparent contradictions must be accepted at face value, for it must not be forgotten that while sceptred monarchs had the right to command, the story-teller's lyre was in the hands of the common people, and clashes were inevitable. It is significant that while rulers are depicted as being the equals of Ares in power and daring, the singer-poets did not create a single myth in which the god of war emerges victorious, but many in which he suffers defeat and humiliation.

As for the illustrations, we believe that a picture should speak for itself. Nevertheless, we should like to say a few words about them.

We had to choose between two schools of thought. According to the one —and this is a line taken by many illustrators— we would have been obliged to remain faithful to the classical originals, chiefly vase-paintings, working in two dimensions, without perspective and with sparing use of colour. The other approach dictated that we use a modern style, and this we have preferred — but with one important prerequisite: that the picture, like the text, must itself be mythology. Thus, while keeping to the classical line, we have added a few elements of perspective where this seemed absolutely necessary. In one respect, however, we felt that we must have absolute freedom, and that was in the colouring. In our opinion, it was precisely the bright colours we have used which would give our work the fairytale air which the myths have to the modern reader's eye. For the ancients, in contrast, mythology was religion. For them the gods were real and not mythical beings. To us mythology is something else — a collection of wise and charming stories which shine like a bright fabric of the imagination from out of the depths of the centuries. It is for this reason that we have tried to illustrate this series with colour alone, or rather, by weaving harmonious contrasts of colour, but never forgetting that our theme is Greek mythology.